Testi

This strange story began two summers ago, when I went to Glacier Park and spent several days at Lake McDonald Lodge. The first day I was there, I took a cruise on the lake. At the end of the cruise I saw that someone had left a leather folder on the boat. I paid it little attention, but I did remember it.

A couple of days later, when I was getting off one of the tourist buses—called Jammers—I saw the same folder on one of the seats. I told the driver about it, and he thanked me.

Late the following night, I was sitting in front of the fireplace at the lodge and saw a folder lying on a nearby chair. I picked it up and realized it was the same folder I had seen two other times. I thought it was odd that the folder seemed to be following me around. I opened it but could find no name or references anywhere in it. I saw that it was a poem but did not try to read it.

I told the night clerk about the folder, and he said that he had seen it on the chair the night before. He said he would keep it at the front desk in case anyone came back for it.

A couple of days later, the night clerk mentioned that no one had picked up the folder and that he was going to throw it away. He asked me if I wanted it, and I told him yes. I gave him my address and phone number in case anyone wanted to contact me about it.

When I got home in about a week, I opened it up and read the poem. It seemed to be more than a first draft, and there was very little wrong with it. I made a couple of spelling changes, but that was all. As I said before, it seemed a little odd that the folder kept following me around. After I read the poem, it seemed even stranger.

This is the poem.

The Ghost of Lake McDonald
Or
The Night Clerk's Tale

Written by Joel Coke

Socdollager

The Ghost of Lake McDonald
Or
The Night Clerk's Tale

The Ghost of Lake McDonald

or

The Night Clerk's Tale

I

Most who come to Lake McDonald have never heard the tale
About two erstwhile lovers who were murdered to no avail.

This tale involved an interloper who stumbled on the truth
As he stayed at Lake McDonald when he was just a youth.

In 1969 it was, when he came to work that summer.
He was tired of studying, and college was a bummer.

His job was that of night clerk, and he mostly worked alone
But he really liked the solitude and made the work his own.

It was said that odd things happened within the lodge at night.
There were ghostly tales of mystery best told by candlelight.

He paid them no attention and concentrated on his work,
To do his job the best he could as a nighttime hotel clerk.

Another winter McDonald Lodge had gracefully survived.
The lodge had yet to open up, and no tourists had arrived.

The night was void of relevance, and boredom was complete.
The lodge was totally empty and with loneliness was replete.

The lobby was quiet and moribund in darkness of the night.
The night clerk heard the fire crackle as logs there did ignite.

Animal heads adorned the walls of the big, well-timbered room
And high above the night clerk's desk, a moose's head did loom.

Surrounded by high balconies in a rustic northwest splendor,
The young man viewed the lobby and the beauty it did render.

As he sat at a night clerk's desk and did a night clerk's work,
He grew tired of the dreary job and became encased in murk.

After working hard for many hours, his work he did forswear
And strode out to the lodge's porch to sit in a rocking chair.

Mist and rain had passed away, and night had totally cleared
And as the clouds were parted, the moon and stars appeared.

As he thought of McDonald Lodge and the local history,
The lake was tranquil, dark, and cool and full of mystery.

2

The beauty of the night and lake he watched in contemplation
And found out he was drawn to them in a powerful temptation.

As he watched the pretty lake, he heard a euphonious sound
That had the lilt of vintage music, and its beauty did abound.

It sounded like a phonograph of the old-time vintage kind.
He listened with astonishment while the music did unwind.

The melodious music, good enough to convey a siren's song,
Called to him and tempted him in a manner deep and strong.

He sought to find the origin of the vintage music playing
But when it wasn't located, he found his state dismaying.

He left his chair and walked about to try to explain the sound
As it came from he knew not where, and its oddness did astound.

From atop the steps he went down and stood beside the lake
And there he found an eerie wonder of which he did partake.

From across the lake there was a voice that he could not deny;
In the lurid light of the fainting moon he heard a distant cry.

Upon the lakeside shore he stood and gazed into the night
As he scanned the sky above and saw an incredible sight.

A shaft of light shot from the moon and fell upon the lake
And revealed a walking woman and a barely visible wake.

As music played in a fetching way that he could not ignore
She came across the glowing water and headed for the shore.

From the edge of Lake McDonald he watched the vision there:
A pretty woman in Victorian dress with long and flowing hair.

The woman stood upon the lake while he watched and reckoned.
Her moving arms and comely eyes called to him and beckoned.

The woman was bewitching, but with a look of much chagrin.
Come here, come here, she seemed to say over and over again

The oddness of the pretty lady was beyond his understanding
Though the request that she made was decidedly commanding.

He watched the woman wave goodbye, then sink beneath the lake
While a sense of what was going on was more than he could make.

Like a siren she enchanted him, and he was drawn to her.
He was greatly tempted with a request he couldn't defer.

In the night he strode the dock and released the rowboat's tie
Then stepped into the wooden boat beneath the starry sky.

The moon was out, the sky was clear, and the water was serene
As he prepared to search the lake to see what he might glean.

From the dock he pulled away with wooden rowboat's oars
As he watched the fading lights of Lake McDonald's shores.

He rowed the boat with little skill, but rowed it well with zest.
Then as he moved, across the water, he never stopped to rest.

While a cold wind blew across the lake, it made him realize
That as he looked into the sky, some storm clouds did arise.

Storm clouds that were in the sky had chased the moon away
While twinkling stars had disappeared behind the dark array.

The starry sky had turned to black, and wind began to blow
While waves arose across the lake as he continued to row.

Rising wind increased the waves and quickly raised his fears
To a level of great anxiety not seen throughout his years.

The rain was blowing sideways, and the boat was turned around
As lightning spiders streaked the sky and thunder was unbound.

When water splashed above the rail and fell into the boat
He hoped that he could do enough to keep himself afloat.

He pulled the oars and rowed ahead to try to increase his speed
But wind blew hard against him as the storm did there impede.

He struggled on, but whirled around and lost his sense of direction.
He rowed upon a storm-tossed wave and tried to make correction.

Lightning struck down from the sky and made the water boil
While rain fell hard across the lake while he did row and moil.

As the boatman rowed, he saw within the rowboat's vanishing wake
A flickering, swirling mass arise from the depths of the stormy lake.

A hand reached from a peaking wave and held the wooden oar
Then a face arose from the stormy lake, covered in grisly gore.

In a fusillade of fantasy that quickly was unveiled
Swaddled with vague reality, the apparition wailed.

He was completely frightened and couldn't believe his eyes
While a bloody, silent, and eerie woman began to slowly rise.

She arose from the windy lake with a blue and eerie light
Wearing a gossamer flowing dress of dazzling, shining white.

A log chain wrapped around her carried a deal of weight
And while he watched her rising, his fear could not abate.

While his heart was beating fast and high up in his throat,
She stood upon the rolling waves beside his rocking boat.

When he watched the blood flow from her severed neck
He fought to keep his sanity and hold his mind in check.

She stepped into the wooden boat and sat down on the seat
And cleaned herself until her face was pretty, soft, and sweet.

He sat in the boat and trembled, too terrified to speak
And felt the horror's presence in circumstances bleak.

As he looked into the face of the horror that stared him down
He felt like jumping overboard but feared that he might drown.

While rain fell all about them, thunder above them broke
And with another bolt of lightning, the apparition spoke.

She spoke to him in a ghostly way as her lengthy hair did blow:
"My given name is Clementine, and I was killed here long ago.

When a man named Harrison killed me and put me in the water,
That was the last that ever was of the socialite's pretty daughter.

I come to you to seek your help for things I cannot do.
I need someone to intervene, and hope that one is you.

Help me, please, I need your help to put my soul at rest
And stop my bouts of misery with which I do contest.

I need someone to find my man and bring us both together
So that we can be united and enhance our romantic tether.

For many years I've suffered pain that I hope I might allay
Yet within this gothic, afflicted realm is where I have to stay.

There's a burden on my soul, but this lake I cannot leave.
Here my very bones are laid, but to love I want to cleave."

With a hopeful, pitiful appearance that was obvious to see
She slowly stepped out of the boat and left her wistful plea.

She walked across the stormy lake with an aura around her form
As she moved across the water within the blasting, howling storm.

While the thunder above the windy lake made its eerie roar,
The walking apparition moved on toward McDonald's shore.

Clementine stood before the lodge as lightning played about.
She called, "I love you, David!" in a strong but plaintive shout.

She spread her arms above her head in an arc of lovely grace
Then sank beneath the rambling waves without a single trace.

II

With his head upon his desk, he awoke the following morn.
With dreams and visions of the night he was quite forlorn.

If things he'd seen were true or false, he knew not as of yet,
But as he went into his room, his shoes and socks were wet.

Was what he'd seen the night before real or just illusion?
He thought about it all the day but came to no conclusion.

Within his mind no answers came as he analyzed his plight,
Thinking about the wonderment he'd known the previous night.

Upon the lake he gazed all day and wondered what he'd seen.
He tried to find some answers and sought what he could glean.

No questions he had were answered, and he gave up the search.
It made him feel like Lake McDonald had left him in the lurch.

III

In the lodge the following night, when he was all alone,
From a couch he saw the fire within the chiseled stone.

The fireplace stood over six feet tall and over twelve feet wide,
An intriguing niche for firewood or a place for a ghost to hide.

The night clerk saw and stared into each shining, burning ember.
There was nothing in the fireplace that reason could remember.

While fiery flakes began to fall in rhythmic repetition,
Within his mind there occurred a wicked premonition.

He watched the burning logs that within the fire did break
Then imagined evil omens with each fiery, flaming flake.

He would gather wood occasionally and feed the fire in snatches,
And each time he'd stop and look at Charlie Russell's scratches.

Upon the dogs he heaped more wood, for it was his desire
To bring about blazing beauty by creating a roaring fire.

The night clerk looked into the fire and saw the glowing blaze.
He watched through burning embers with a penetrating gaze.

Sap was sizzling in the fire and made an occasional pop
As fiery logs burned apart and pieces of them did drop.

8

The clerk was alone at three a.m. at Lake McDonald Lodge
And sat at ease upon a couch as work he tried to dodge.

When a fiery log broke in half and sparks flew through the air,
They congregated on sooty stones after flying there.

They moved across the sooty black in a brief, determined sweep
That reminded him quite readily of a flock of grazing sheep.

The fiery sparks mixed with smut and started a crimson line
That marched across the fireplace wall as if by great design.

The pretty sparks became aligned, and a circle was arrayed.
The crimson circle expanded, and a vision there was made.

While he watched, he saw a face behind the flaming fire
Upon a stone, above a log, where smoke was rising higher.

He stared at it and couldn't believe the amazing thing he saw.
"It's a configuration of carbon black or a stone that has a flaw.

It's strangeness in the stonework, but it's only crumbling grout.
It's not a face—it just looks like one. It's nothing to worry about."

He stared at it and marveled well and found himself in awe
Of the image that was created and revealed as what he saw.

He watched again the roving sparks to see what they might reap
While they once again reminded him of a flock of grazing sheep.

After a while the visions came, and he watched them all in awe
Of all the things that were revealed in the embers that he saw.

Within the vision a young girl stood upon the rippling lake
While all around the glowing fire, the embers there did flake.

It seemed to him that words were made within the sooty black.
The clinging sparks were crimson, and their beauty didn't lack.

9

The night clerk watched as sparks arrayed upon the fireplace stone
Where words like seeds upon the rocks were there so brightly sown.

She's in the lake, she's in the lake, is what the message said.
She's on the bottom of Lake McDonald, lying pitifully dead.

A ghostly cry for help was heard from within the flaming fire
That sounded like a person troubled, in circumstances dire.

The night clerk stared at the crimson words and had a revelation,
Yet within his mind he searched around and found no validation.

His attempts at understanding were punctuated by bad luck
While thoughts within his churning mind began to run amok.

"The things I hear and things I see are all things quite surreal
But they're only ploys of trickery, and none of them are real."

The clerk grew tired of fireplace faces and attacks upon his reason,
So he decided not to worry and thought of the tourist season.

He watched the fiery embers in each falling, tumbling flake
While reality came relentlessly and gave his mind a shake.

A log broke down, and sparks flew up and hit the sooty stones
And were arranged before him as dismembered, broken bones.

He threw it away out of his thoughts as just a configuration.
"It's nothing more than soot stains inflamed by imagination."

In a moment the face returned and stared out through the fire.
The night clerk felt that what he watched made his sight a liar.

"It's nothing but a simulacrum. It's really nothing at all.
It's only a representation of a face on the fireplace wall."

But as he stared and stared again, it seemed to come to life.
As he watched in amazement, his thoughts were running rife.

He stared into the embers and a movement did discern
While the fiery, rising vision caused him great concern.

The image he saw transformed itself into blazing clarity
Then raised itself from the fireplace as a blazing verity.

A log blew up in the fireplace near the back of the big rock wall.
Then a plume of flame arose from the fire, standing six feet tall.

The fiery image of a burning man walked from the fireplace
And stood before the night clerk and looked into his face.

With flaming eyes he engaged the clerk and held onto his mind.
He communicated without words but with meaning well defined.

The night clerk backed away from him, but didn't run and hide.
He stood his ground and held his own and with terror did abide.

The vision stood with burning eyes and horror unrefined.
He bade the clerk to follow him and leave the room behind.

"I'll take you to my burial place from which I might arise.
You'll dig my bones and carry them to where my lover lies.

What's left of me is ashes and broken bits of blackened bone.
They're buried out in the forest underneath an errant stone.

Now come on here and follow me, and we'll go to my grave
Where you can find and take my ashes to the one I crave."

The night clerk looked at the vision and felt both weak and hollow,
But he remembered the previous night and felt that he must follow.

The vision walked out through the door beyond an employee dorm
As the night clerk rose from his couch and followed the fiery form.

Through the woods the vision went in a way that did astound.
He seemed to float within the air while he did leap and bound.

11

The night clerk walked behind, but stumbled often and fell.
He tore his jacket, bruised his leg, and once gave out a yell.

They walked the woods to a little glade within the forest night
And the glade as the moon shone down was a welcome sight.

The vision stood beside a log and pointed toward a rock
To tell him that beneath the stone was a mystery to unlock.

As wind came up within the night, evergreens were swayed.
Again he pointed to the rock, where shadows were arrayed.

"Dig here," he spoke. "It's under this rock that my remains were laid.
Harrison buried my blackened bones within this moonlit glade.

I want my bones to be removed and scattered across the lake.
Now I ask that you take a boat and throw them in its wake.

I hope that there they will embrace the bones of Clementine
So that our souls can come together and happily intertwine."

With sadness in the vision's face that he could not disguise,
He well remembered Clementine and spoke of her demise.

The firedrops in his haunted eyes made the clerk agree
To help the flaming vision and yield to his plaintive plea.

The vision pointed to the rock that was by moonlight shaded
And while the night clerk watched, the burning vision faded.

Suddenly the clerk awakened, with all the visions gone.
The room was getting bright, for it was breaking dawn.

The night clerk wondered fervently of things he did review
As he asked himself repeatedly if what he'd seen was true.

Then on his person what he found was difficult to ignore,
For he had torn his jacket and had bruises by the score.

IV

Once again on the following night, the clerk began to tire.
He readily left his boring job and began to tend the fire.

More logs were thrown upon the fire to heat it even hotter.
The last one waved upon the pile like a blazing teeter-totter.

The fire was popping loudly, and suddenly there was a blast.
Debris and sparks rose in the air and on the floor were cast.

A log broke down within the fire, and sparks flew in the air.
The night clerk saw the broken wood as it was burning there.

He took an interesting book that he'd never had time to read
And he started to turn the pages with all deliberate speed.

There by the fire the night clerk sat and read his book alone
When from above and to his left he heard a plaintive moan.

At first he paid no attention, and the sound was just ignored
So he continued to read his book with his ignorance restored.

Then again a sound was heard that seemed to be a moan,
A plaintive, pitiful, painful sound like none he'd ever known.

He slowly turned his head and looked to the third-floor railing
In the direction of the place from which the sound was hailing.

While the thoughts within his mind were spinning like a fan,
Across the room the night clerk saw a choking, hanging man.

Struggling at the end of a rope, the poor man slowly dangled,
Hanging by a broken neck, harshly stretched and mangled.

The man was swaying slightly, and his face was quite contorted.
His neck was broken viciously where the deadly rope cavorted.

The clerk was stunned and mesmerized and in rapt fixation
While he strained to overcome his abject blind prostration.

He couldn't believe the reality of the horror at which he peered
So he closed his eyes to hide the view of an image that he feared.

After a moment he looked again and found himself relieved,
For he found that awful vision could no longer be perceived.

The haunting vision was gone and wasn't to be seen.
Emptiness of the balcony was all that he could glean.

While beautiful Kainai lanterns hung from the lobby's ceiling,
The night clerk was confused, and his mind was swiftly reeling.

He looked around, but nothing there seemed to be awry,
Though something odd had happened that he couldn't deny.

In a moment he looked again, but the vision wasn't there.
He concluded that it was best to forget the whole affair.

"The things I hear and things I see are all things quite surreal,
But they're only ploys of trickery, and none of them are real."

He laughed out loud, shook his head, and broke out in a grin,
Then sat back down upon the couch and began to read again.

After a while, when he'd forgotten the vision that he'd seen,
He was engrossed within a book whose plot he tried to glean.

He sat there reading peacefully and was totally unconcerned
As something in the fireplace suddenly snapped and burned.

A sudden touch of unknown stealth caused the clerk to yell.
He stood and saw an apparition straight from a living hell.

With a noose around his broken neck, a horrid man did stand.
He had a swollen, tortured face and a rope coiled in his hand.

The night clerk covered his eyes and turned his head around
For what he'd seen with his own eyes certainly did astound.

He removed his hands, rubbed his eyes, then he felt forsaken,
For what he saw before him there left him totally shaken.

With a revelation of consciousness beyond what should be known
He was fraught with fear and trembling that he could not disown.

He saw the form of the ghostly man standing in the room,
Bringing about a terrible fear that he could not subsume.

"Who are you?" the night clerk yelled and quickly backed away.
He held his hands in front of his face to keep the thing at bay.

The man of broken countenance said to the frightened clerk,
"There is no need to run from me or act like you're berserk.

There is no need to fear me, though I seem a dreadful sight.
Please sit with me and hear me out upon this dreary night.

I ask your kind indulgence and do not wish you harm.
Please, just sit and listen. There's no need for your alarm.

My name is Harrison Taylor, and I'm in bleak despair,
For I am but a fugitive from memory's harshest glare.

The things you've seen recently are more than vivid dreams.
They represent harsh reality, which is greater than it seems.

It was years ago on a pristine night when my fate was set,
Creating all the future pain that my treachery did beget.

It's been many years since I died, yet memory does enslave,
For the evil I made long ago sends guilt beyond the grave.

I was driven to rampant madness of a monomaniacal style
In which only a man of evil could conceive of things so vile.

I took two people's lives and thereby ruined my own,
And as a ghost I walk these halls in anguish all alone.

I was driven to awful madness by a woman that I adored
To do things of great iniquity that eventually I abhorred.

I put her body into the lake, where its remnants linger yet,
And from that time until this time with guilt I've been beset.

I seek to find a little comfort, as my soul is vastly taxed,
For over time, since my death, my pain has greatly waxed.

The things you've seen and heard are pitiful cries for help
To seek relief from circumstance that I did bring to whelp.

I'll explain everything that happened in every vile detail
In hopes that when you hear me, your kindness will avail."

V

"In a time of demonic passion I took two people's lives,
And just their ghostly memory is all that now survives.

It's a story of terrible vengeance that I have now to tell
About exorcising a demon that in my mind did dwell.

I tried to destroy their love by taking away their lives.
Now my guilt from iniquity is why my anguish thrives.

The story began in 1912 but hasn't been told till now.
It's a secret held for many years that here I do avow.

I was to marry my Clementine, who came from Eastern means,
Whose father made a goodly fortune with industrial machines.

Her parents both were socialites of the utmost wealthy kind,
And the future of young Clementine had been well designed.

The parties and the baubles of the wounded Gilded Age
Were all very transparent but still seemed all the rage.

16

I was a man of the Ivy League with a glittering life ahead,
Sired in a wealthy family, well placed, and very well bred.

I was apprenticed to an architect to learn a gentleman's trade
With a desire to design and build that no one could dissuade.

I left the East for Lake McDonald after my last school term
Where I was given a new position in an architectural firm.

The firm was chosen to build a lodge upon McDonald's lake.
My journey across the continent was one I was glad to make.

For many months I worked hard to learn my new profession.
It didn't take but a little while till work was a great obsession.

In early spring, as work began with weather being better,
From my bride-to-be Miss Clementine I received a letter.

Clementine was a suffragette with everything that meant
And made a stunning proposition in a letter that she sent.

Clementine thought Montana was very much a place of note
And said she wanted to see it, for here she could probably vote.

I told her not to come alone, for it wouldn't seem so right.
She wrote to me very quickly, and as usual was forthright.

She laughed at my suggestions and said to be on time
For when she arrived by train, it wouldn't be a crime.

To see her man at Lake McDonald was her bold intention.
Clementine knew her mind and cared not for convention.

Clementine was a willful girl, but I loved her all the more.
I was alone at Lake McDonald and, missing her, was sore.

She was as bold as I expected, as I quickly did surmise,
For Clementine came all by herself, not to my surprise.

I met her there when she arrived at the Whitefish Station
For she had traveled all alone well over half the nation.

I gave her a wind-up phonograph as a special arrival gift.
With a kiss upon my cheek, her thanks was fine and swift.

Though she hadn't been there but a month or a little more,
She found the area beautiful, and the lodge she did adore.

Clementine was interested in the building of the fine hotel.
She got an idea in her pretty head that no one could dispel.

She wanted to marry in the new hotel with invitees as guests,
Planning the wedding meticulously with all that love suggests.

She wanted a wedding reception at a gathering by the lake
Where our families and friends and all there could partake.

I acquiesced to every wish that she wanted to divulge
To bring about a happiness that we could both indulge.

VI

As work on the new McDonald Lodge had been mostly finished,
The needed number of workers had been somewhat diminished.

From Kalispell a mason came who worked his trade alone.
His job was to make a fireplace of rough-cut quarried stone.

As I watched the construction of the fireplace being made,
My Clementine accompanied me to see the place displayed.

Clementine noticed the mason while she wore a leather skirt.
Then, when I had left the building, I felt that she tried to flirt.

She was taken by the rustic lad who set her soul to fly.
Clementine would see him later certainly, bye and bye.

David was a tradesman who moiled his hands in stone,
A tough-as-leather working man of raw sinew and bone.

To the brawny, vigorous, burnished youth with wavy, sandy hair
Clementine was much attracted as she saw him working there.

A couple of times when I was away, my Clementine came alone
To see the brown-haired mason who worked in quarried stone.

Their first few conversations were staid and rather mundane,
But affection grew between them that they could not contain.

Clementine watched him work whenever she felt she could.
Inside the room, across the floor, she sat or silently stood.

With whatever aesthetics that David had envisioned
The stones were fitted and were greatly precisioned.

While Clementine watched those stones being placed,
She hoped for his touch in which love would be laced.

Clementine watched him rive the rocks as she stood alone.
After a while in his presence, she felt like a breaking stone.

As she watched the mason work, she was kept alert
By the moving muscularity beneath his denim shirt.

Clementine watched the mason as her young heart soared
And concluded that the workman was a man to be adored.

Across the floor the young man walked, and by her he did stand.
He placed his glove upon the stone and took her proffered hand.

To each other across the room their hearts were wildly driven.
Within his arms she was kissed and felt like stone being riven.

Swept away by the rabble love of a workman at his trade,
The wants and wiles of affection for her fiancé did fade.

Against her will and reservation, she was taken away by chance
While her satisfaction and happiness did quickly there advance.

It was as a wind so wildly blown that no one could withstand,
Or a swirling leaf in a hurricane, not knowing where to land.

The rabble wind on a restless night conveyed her strong desire
That fell upon the workman's soul and filled him full of fire.

Clementine felt like a mighty river cascading over a fall.
She knew that she needed rescue, but didn't care to call.

Clementine had a decision to make and would make it all alone:
It was a man from the Ivy League, or one who worked in stone.

With that moment in reality she manifested her intention
To leave her wealthy fiancé and break with all convention.

Though it took me a little time, I finally became suspicious,
For Clementine, the suffragette, was somewhat injudicious.

It was after investigation that I found I wanted to act,
For I feared I could turn suspicion into an actual fact.

I planned a trap for Clementine and planned it very well,
Then told her I had a meeting and was going to Kalispell.

Clementine happily smiled and willingly took the bait
Then went and told her David, because she couldn't wait.

'Harrison is going to Kalispell and will be gone all day.
We can come and be together while Harrison is away.'

David was delighted while he planned with Clementine.
She smiled at him and giggled as they cheated by design.

'You meet me here tomorrow noon, when I will be alone.
You can come and be with me while I work the stone.'

Clementine went to David on the following afternoon
In hopes that in the lodge alone they might there commune.

Clementine brought a picnic lunch and something in a box.
She put her basket on the top of one of the quarried blocks.

She took from the box the phonograph and placed it on a table
While a place was cleared for the phonograph to make it very stable.

Clementine wound her phonograph so that it would run,
Then brought out many records to play them just for fun.

She happily took those records and put them on display.
'Let Me Call You Sweetheart' was what she chose to play.

This was the song she often heard as phonographs were played.
She sang the song to her rabble love as they danced and swayed.

The phonograph played the music as rapture was enhanced
And Clementine sang the song while the couple happily danced.

She used a wind-up phonograph to dance with her rabble love
And while he held her in his arms, she fit like a beautiful glove.

David held his Clementine while he stroked her chestnut hair.
Then he pulled his lady close, and he kissed her dancing there.

With beautiful fire burning there in hot and broad revue
Smoke and sparks were created and up the chimney flew.

Taken away like a boat at flood, she couldn't control the drift.
The artisan who worked in stone had caused a passionate rift.

Swept away to uncharted realms, she couldn't avoid his touch
Then fell into enchanted wonder which she enjoyed so much.

With a grasp as strong as grappling rope, he took her in embrace
Then with a touch like morning mist, he kissed her waiting face.

21

He threw her on a block of stone and kissed her where she lay
And while she felt his heated love, her mind did dance and play.

At summer's eve her body lay on the coolness of the stone
And quivered there in reality of a love so brightly shown.

He carried her to wondrous places she'd never been before,
Then after her sweet surrender, she was given even more

They didn't know that I was hidden behind the lodge's walls
And witnessed things the lovers did, in all that hate enthralls.

I saw them through a window as they were dancing there
While they engaged in sweet embrace without a single care.

I watched as David, the working man, held my sweetheart well
And as I saw them dancing there, I wished them both in hell.

In my mind there burned an image of those lovers in embrace
And my fists were clenched in rage as I pondered my disgrace.

I watched them from a hiding place as my hate began to seethe
As turmoil swirling inside my mind caused my soul to wreathe.

I wanted to break in on them while I watched them dance
And kill them with alacrity without giving them a chance.

I refrained from killing them, yet imagined sweet revenge.
But while I watched the lovers kiss, I felt my mind unhinge.

I saw my happy Clementine in the room with the rustic lad
And while I watched, I hated him with all the hate I had.

It mattered not how the high cost, and it mattered not the sin.
By then I was driven completely mad to do my challenger in.

The given love of a working man was greater than my own,
Brought about in a single summer by seeds so briefly sown.

I was completely mortified at the hands of the local lad
And thought I'd been mistreated in a manner very bad.

As my money and my society were spurned by Clementine,
All my hopes and dreams with her were broken by design.

My visions of my Clementine in the arms of a rabble love
Caused my demons to unwind and gave my mind a shove.

I was consumed by madness and impaled upon revenge.
I made arrangements carefully so wrong I could avenge.

I sought my vengeance eagerly and came up with a plan
To avenge the wrong of Clementine and her working man.

For a couple of weeks I waited and quietly took my time,
But then I found my moment with my hatred in its prime.

After the lodge was finished, there was held a celebration
For the building was at its best and covered in decoration.

It was after an elegant supper when everyone else was gone
That I brought into fruition the revengeful plan I'd drawn.

I held her very closely and I asked my Clementine
To ride across the lake on that pretty night so fine.

'We'll take the wind-up phonograph and play it in the night
While stars are in the sky and the moon is wondrous bright.

We'll listen to some music while the stars above us lie
As we row across the water beneath the mountain sky.'

Clementine feigned some interest and said she'd like to go,
For night was full of wonder and would put on quite a show.

I led my cheating Clementine to the shore and a wooden boat.
She wore her pretty evening dress and a purple evening coat.

Clementine stepped into the boat and sat down upon the seat.
The phonograph lay in the floor, while treachery was replete.

I pushed the rowboat from the dock, and then I took the oars.
We pulled away into the lake as we left McDonald's shores.

As I rowed across the water throughout the waiting night,
The stars were hanging in the sky like ornaments of light.

The silver moon reflected well on the surface of the lake
As I silently rowed the rowboat and left a shining wake.

When I stopped my silent rowing, we drifted on the water.
Within the silver moonlight I saw the socialite's daughter.

Like a pristine maiden in moonlight in a beatific array,
Her face and form were beautiful in wonderful display.

She looked like an actual angel and took my breath away
And back from my vile intention I started slowly to sway.

I could have been forgiving, even through great chagrin.
Maybe there was a chance I hoped to win her love again.

I loved her, so I wanted her and was willing to forgive
And was willing to marry her, with all my love to give.

I almost couldn't go on, but I steeled my wavering soul.
I thought of her lover, David, and a demon took control.

I firmly looked at Clementine before I spoke my mind.
Then I spoke quite willfully in a manner well defined.

'You took my love and battered it till it was badly broken,
Then took my heart quite willingly and used it for a token.'

In spite of hell's encroachment, I gave her one last chance.
I hoped she'd say she wanted me and break my evil trance.

'You've been unfaithful, Clementine, and that I can't allow.
Clementine, do you still love me? I want your answer now.'

Clementine sat silently as she watched the moon's reflection.
Then she slowly turned to me to reveal her heart's direction.

With risen eyes she met the stare of a most unhappy man.
She looked at me quite sadly and revealed a heartfelt plan.

'Harrison, you are wonderful, with an affection sweet and kind.
I was delighted to be your wife and to that was well resigned.

Harrison, what I'll say to you now hurts me to the core.
It's not that I don't love you, it's just I love him more.

The things you offer abundantly are things I've always had.
He offers things I've never known that seem to drive me mad.

With David I feel more alive than at any time I can remember.
I want to spend my life with him and flame as a burning ember.

I had no intention when I came to alter my well-planned life.
Harrison, you're an excellent man and can find another wife.

Hopefully we'll part as friends and leave bad things behind.
There is no reason for either of us to hate or feel maligned.'

I sat in the rowboat silently and never replied at all
While over Lake McDonald there seemed to hang a pall.

I felt I was possessed, and with all other options gone,
I knew I'd been betrayed and became a devil's pawn.

I turned around and placed a record upon the phonograph.
'Let Me Call You Sweetheart' I played with a little laugh.

'After listening to your treachery, of which I'm in receipt,
I play this wind-up phonograph upon the rowboat's seat.

The song I play is the one you used to share a sweet embrace.
I play it now, for you have come and betrayed me to my face.'

I reached into my pocket and retrieved a shaving razor,
Then smiled while I held it up like a simple party favor.

I stood before sweet Clementine while the rowboat rocked
And when I took her by the neck, Clementine was shocked.

I roughly pulled her auburn hair and sadistically did gloat
As I took my steel straight razor and slit her pretty throat.

Blood shot from her mangled neck and landed in the water
And there I took the life of the socialite's pretty daughter.

I wrapped her in a log chain and laughed across the night
Then lowered her body into the water within the lunar light.

Blood mingled with the pristine water and dissipated well.
The body slowly floated downward and to the bottom fell.

Clementine's mouth was open for a scream she never made.
Now she lies quite silently, with her whitened bones arrayed.

While I stood in the rowboat and cleaned my bloody blade,
'Let Me Call You Sweetheart' was the music being played.

Above the final resting place of the socialite's pretty daughter
I stood up within the rowboat and looked down into the water.

I held the playing phonograph and spoke to my Clementine,
And while I did, my voice and music did surreally intertwine.

'I thought that it would be fitting for you to hear your song,
So now when you play this phonograph, you can sing along.'

While the phonograph was playing, I threw it into the lake.
'I think you'll like this music that you can endlessly partake.'

After cleaning Clementine's blood from the rowboat's floor,
I turned the boat around and went toward McDonald's shore.

The things I offered Clementine were those of a rich man's creed
But what I offered she didn't want and seemed to have no need.

She took the love of an artisan who used his hands in stone
And though I offered the best I had, she left my love alone.

While rowing back, I thought about the killing of Clementine
And felt David was responsible and would be the next in line.

It was to the rabble workman that I shifted my great guilt
For my hatred for the young man was far beyond the hilt.

Deep within my haunted mind, my soul broke down and cried
For I knew it was the mason's fault that Clementine had died.

I went and called the mason from the quarters where he slept
Then took him to the lodge where inside the door we stepped.

We stood beside the fireplace while reddened embers faded
And I yelled in David's face as my hatred was pervaded.

'You stole my lady's affection, and I'm here to ask you why.
Clementine was to marry me and was the apple of my eye.'

David the workman looked at me and didn't even flinch,
And when he gave his explanation, he didn't give an inch.

'Clementine is in love with me, and now she is my own.
Our love is one of majesty that you will not dethrone.

I never stole your Clementine—she readily came to me.
She was in a rich man's cage, and I gladly set her free.

I am enthralled with Clementine, and we will marry well.
I'll build a house all by myself, and we'll live in Kalispell.'

'I can assure you beyond all doubt that this will not occur.
There is no way this side of hell you'll ever marry her.

Clementine lies dead at the bottom of McDonald's lake.
I was pleased to kill her, for it was me she did forsake.

It's you that made me murder, and it's you who is to blame.
You have made this madness, and you have made this shame.'

I screamed at Clementine's lover in a vile, definitive screed,
Then hit him with a rod of iron I'd brought for such a need.

I took the mason's hammer and smashed the mason's head,
Then beat his body mercilessly till the mason fell near dead.

I was fraught with bellicosity and couldn't control my rage
While I turned Lake McDonald Lodge into a vicious stage.

David lay across the floor with blood all over the place
Yet yelled with his broken jaw from his damaged face:

'It matters not whether you rant or kill me as you rave.
The love I have for Clementine exists beyond the grave.

You'll never take our love away, though you've killed us both.
No matter what you do with us, you'll never break our troth.'

David's love for his pretty Clementine could never be denied,
And with defiance in his fading eyes, Clementine's lover died.

VII

I thought that it was proper and fitting to use the fireplace
So I could burn the evidence and hide my bitter disgrace.

I threw some sawn-up timbers upon those fireplace dogs
And placed the body of the mason upon the pile of logs.

It was then with great alacrity, in an act of sound dispatch,
I poured kerosene all over the lot and lit it with a match.

In an effort to ruin the evidence, as was my great desire,
I created around David's body a ripping, roaring fire.

Flames arose in the fireplace and brought a roaring sound
While harsh revenge and infamy did everywhere abound.

Though I knew that it was wrong and might lead me to hell,
I had taken my sweet revenge and had savored it very well.

I laughed at the workman's body as it burned away and crackled
As stones of the great fireplace with sizzling blood were spackled.

Devoid of all humanity, I burned David's body there.
It was then I felt triumphant and had no sense to care.

I placed more wood in the fireplace, and it continued to kindle
While the body kept on burning and continued there to dwindle.

I watched the ashes constantly and stirred them many times
Then burned the ashes once again to hide my vicious crimes.

Except for the blackened skull, there was little there but ashes.
Nothing was left upon the stones but grayish bloody splashes.

I shoveled the ashes into a bucket, along with splintered bones
And put it on the fireplace hearth where David laid the stones.

It was after I'd filled the bucket up that I decided to stop.
Then I took those awful ashes with David's skull on top.

It was a bucket of grayish ashes with broken, blackened bones
That I carried from the fireplace made out of chiseled stones.

Within the haunted darkness where I in stealth did creep
I dug a hole in the forest, and with a shovel I dug it deep.

I stomped the shovel into the ground and dug out earth in hunks
That I cast far away from me, where they fell with heavy plunks.

At three feet deep and one foot wide, the hole was then complete.
Down in the hole I threw the ashes that I was trying to secrete.

Using a stone repeatedly, I smashed the workman's skull
With a manner of utter viciousness too brutal now to mull.

When I had destroyed the skull of the poor, unfortunate youth,
I kicked the shards into the grave to hide the horrible truth.

I threw the dirt back in the hole, where it fell with a flop,
Then covered the hole with leaves and leveled out its top.

I rolled a rock atop the hole and created a hiding place
That only I and no one else would ever be able to trace.

VIII

It didn't take long for folks to find that Clementine was gone
While as for me, I happily played the part of a pitiful pawn.

If asked about my Clementine, what I always did was scoff:
She fell for a low-class workman, and they had both run off.

'Good riddance,' I told the people. 'She was just that kind.
I'll get on with the rest of life and leave the past behind.

She was a little strumpet, and I'm glad I found her out.
I'm better off without her, and of that there is no doubt.'

No one seemed to question me about the things I said,
For with rumors of illicit love, no one felt them dead.

The brave façade that I presented was never really believed.
They thought I was devastated and treacherously deceived.

After the lodge was finished, I stayed around for a time.
I thought that the great betrayal had justified my crime.

It wasn't long before I found that I'd fallen in despair.
My conscience got the best of me, far beyond compare.

All my plans for happiness had literally turned to grief.
Now there was nothing left for me, except to find relief.

After anguishing for many months and seeking absolution,
I then decided to end my life and sought my own solution.

In a way to handle my agony that I finally did deduce,
I took the end of a tackle rope and made of it a noose.

I took the steps of the lodge's stairs as high as falconry
Then I tied the rope to a rail and stood on the balcony.

As I looked down from up on high, my agony was great,
So off the third-floor balcony I jumped and met my fate.

31

I dangled from the railing like a swinging chandelier
While gurgling as I died like a croaking Chanticleer.

I hung like a broken puppet above the lodge's floor
For two long weeks of infamy, enhancing the décor.

It was only by passing fancy that my corpse was discovered
As the ghost of my bloated body around the rafters hovered.

A passing hiker saw me through a random windowpane
And reported what was seen as the horror there did reign.

My body went to New England and was buried near my home,
But my ghost is here at Lake McDonald, where it's free to roam.

The local lore said I hanged myself because I was distraught
About my loss of Clementine and the heartbreak that it wrought.

I hanged myself from a wooden rail, but that's not why I died.
I left this life to ease my guilt and to salve my wounded pride.

There were investigations by Clementine's family and mine
But they concluded it was true about David and Clementine.

Both families were suspicious, but in time they let it go
For they grew tired of looking with no evidence to show.

David had no local family who seemed to care at all.
Most felt that he had followed a benevolent siren's call.

After many diligent searches with many people involved,
The event was hailed as finished but never was resolved.

Still, for a few over the years it has become a mystery
And has entered into the local lore and the local history.

IX

In hopes I could ameliorate or absolve myself of pain,
I successfully killed myself, but my existence is a bane.

It didn't work; it never did. It's worse now than before.
Now my ghostly mind is riveted to things that I abhor.

It's lonely here to be a ghost immersed in past regret
Of evil things and foul mistakes by which I am beset.

Ghosts are very haunted creatures, even as they prey on others.
They are bedeviled by vile events that hobble all their druthers.

Since the time I killed them both, I've felt my pain increase.
I want relief from awful guilt to find my soul some peace.

What I did was terribly wrong, and I must make amends.
I'll prepare myself for eternity and whatever God intends.

I want to put the hearts together of people that I killed
And alleviate the grief I have and see their love fulfilled.

I can't go on, I can't go on and suffer this anymore.
My ghostly soul is heavy and hurts me to the core.

It seemed I was possessed by a great, demonic power.
While well outside my sanity, my integrity did cower.

I killed them both with wanton hate to keep their love apart,
Then I took my life through envy and died of a broken heart.

I know their love still lives, even though they both are dead,
For the love that is between them is held by a mystic thread.

I can readily feel their affection in the fabric of this place
And I know they have a love that my hate could not erase.

Their spirits suffer mightily, and they can't come together,
For powers that inhibit them are too difficult to weather.

If you help me in what I'm asking, then I can play a part
To bring their love together and put them heart to heart.

What their spirits are asking you is all you need to do
And they will come together when the task is through.

If I can bring their spirits together, it might ease my guilt
And ameliorate the consequence of anguish that I've built.

I know well it's not enough and will never make things right.
It's my frail attempt at goodness, as my heart is now contrite.

If you will kindly help me, I'll leave them to their love
And give myself quite willingly to God up high above.

I hope they're reunited, and I wish their spirits well,
For maybe by a loving God I'll avoid the pains of hell."

The night clerk saw silently to the depths of Harrison's eyes
Then kindly spoke to the ghostly figure as he did empathize:

"There's something in your eyes that leads me to believe
You truly want to help them and aren't trying to deceive."

While he watched the crackling, snapping, burning firewood
The clerk replied that he would help and do the best he could.

Harrison seemed in great surprise and almost disbelief
Then lowered his ghostly head with a sigh of fine relief.

"I thank you, sir, for helping me, for it's more than I deserve
As I seek some restitution and some goodness to preserve."

The night clerk turned his head and into the fire did stare.
Then when he looked for Harrison, Harrison wasn't there.

X

As sunlight struck the night clerk, he awoke with an intention
To enact the will of Harrison through benevolent intervention.

The night clerk was convinced that he had a valid calling
Though he knew what he had to do was totally appalling.

Under the moon that very night, he took his shovel in hand
Where beside the rock, beneath the trees, he did take a stand.

There in the midst of silver light he stood before the stone.
With his shovel and digging tool he worked there all alone.

He thought of the ghost the night before and he became inspired,
Then moved the rock and began to dig deep in the place desired.

Behind the mountain, across the lake, a distant thunder rolled
While a pulsing, crawling luminescence of beauty was extolled.

Lightning bolts were neatly sheathed in vast, celestial clouds
Created by the exploding redness of disappearing shrouds.

Waving trees put moving shadows upon the forest ground
And as he looked for the buried bones, eeriness did abound.

With his shovel he began to dig in a shadow beneath a tree.
He dug down deep, and after a while he began to find debris.

Along with blackened bones and a piece of a leather shoe
There was a broken belt buckle with a dusty, darkened hue.

He found the missing body of the unfortunate murdered swain
Where for years in forest ground the blackened bones had lain.

With a bucket of ancient ashes and shards of a broken skull
He went away from David's grave during the thunder's lull.

Around the lodge and down the steps the bucket he did tote
Then put the carried bones and ashes into a wooden boat.

From the dock he rowed the boat into the frothing lake,
Then across the stormy water the wooden oars did rake.

Drawn over Lake McDonald by a powerful unknown force,
The night clerk hoped relentlessly he was going to its source.

He dipped his oar into the water while thunder broke the sky
And went to find the unhappy place where Clementine did lie.

Lightning scarred the darkness and reflected on the water
As he sought the bones of the socialite's murdered daughter.

The falling rain was pelting him like an unrelenting force
Yet he rowed across the water and stayed the fateful course.

He was assaulted by great thunder with long, acoustical lashes
As celestial fire fell to ground with jagged lightning flashes.

He took the boat aggressively to the midst of McDonald's lake
Where he felt a premonition and hoped the storm would break.

Within the thunder's awful sounds and brilliant lightning flashes
Upon the churning lake's black water he threw the bucket's ashes.

In a moment the lake was serene and the surface was like glass
While a feeling fell upon the lake that no wonder could surpass.

Moonlight struck the placid lake that enclosed the wooden boat
And then the worries of the night clerk all seemed quite remote.

The storm was in the distance with thunder's fading sounds.
On the water was a stillness that seemed to know no bounds.

The ashes drifted through the water and there began to darkle
Then floated down within the lake and soon began to sparkle.

Spirits in the moving water seemed richly, wildly blessed
For the sparkles came together and then quickly coalesced.

Deep below the water's surface, a swirling there occurred
And he saw in the swirling water, figures that were blurred.

The ashes began to scintillate and grow increasingly bright
While their ascending luminescence electrified the night.

He looked into the swirling lake and saw an amorphous shape
That rose from the deepest water like a beautiful, flowing cape.

The thing kept turning and spinning as the sparkling did delight
Then rose from the deepest waters and broke the waves at night.

In the lunar light of the pristine night, two figures did emerge.
They were seen by him upon the lake within that ghostly verge.

The light was made of dancing figures of David and Clementine.
As they embraced and twirled together, their souls did intertwine.

They danced on the water in moonlight in an amatory guise
While looking at each other through loving, sparkling eyes.

With the visitation of wonderment that from the depths arose
An enchantment was instilled in him that even now still grows.

He left the dancing spirits and rowed to McDonald's shore
Then walked the lodge's steps on through the lodge's door.

He stood before the fireplace within the great lodge room
As fire still burned atop the dogs to illuminate the gloom.

Harrison's ghost appeared to him and stood before the fire
Then talked to the clerk abundantly about his great desire.

"I watched the dance upon the lake of the reunited souls
That came as a realization and a fulfillment of my goals.

From their fear and desperation I hope they find release.
I give their love a blessing and bow to their sweet peace.

I was never a terrible person until I learned to hate.
It was just my broken love that the devil used as bait.

If I suffer through all eternity, I will deserve no less
But maybe my atonement a righteous God will bless.

I feel no need to linger here, for it's now that I must leave.
It's time I left and met my fate, and to eternity I'll cleave.

I appreciate the help you've given, and now I'll disappear,
For it's now I'll meet my destiny and I'll do it without fear."

While sparks arose in the fireplace and assembled on the stone,
He waved and smiled and disappeared and left the clerk alone.

The night clerk saw the blazing fire as wonder did perform
When an errant batch of fiery sparks turned into a swarm.

Sparks moved upon the stony wall and wandered in fiery herds
Then grazed across the sooty black, arranged in crimson words.

"Thank you" were the written words on the blackened fireplace wall.
They were written there tendentiously in a gleaming crimson scrawl.

As he stood and watched the words, they slowly disappeared
And left a clear and empty stone to which they had adhered

XI

I've told the story as I know it and how it came to be
With its mysterious convolutions, all involving me.

I was the night clerk I talked about in the story that I've told
And all I've said is entirely true, with no fragment left untold.

Now what of the awful murderer whose spirit here did dwell?
I hope at last he's found some peace, and I truly wish him well.

He's suffered pain for many years, but hopefully not forever.
He's paying for his terrible crimes of a past he tried to sever.

I'll think of him occasionally and extend him charity
And hope his pain is lessened as he resides in eternity.

My story is an awful one, but in a way it ends quite well,
So I'll now finish with a flourish the tale I've tried to tell.

Over the years I've often returned to the lodge and pretty lake.
They're a source of inspiration and a place for enjoyment's sake.

They're a hiding place for mysteries and rich romantic lore
So come at night and take a stand on Lake McDonald's shore.

I've heard it said by those who know that much to their delight
A dance takes place on Lake McDonald sometimes in the night.

When moonlight shines upon the lake and water there does glisten,
A love song drifts across the lake and is heard by those who listen.

People don't talk about it much, but it's said that it is true
That after storms upon the lake when starlight does renew

Two figures will at night arise within the moonlight's mist.
They smile and start to dance together after they have kissed.

In lambent light of the crystal night the spirits softly twirl.
They can be seen upon the lake as love does there unfurl.

She in a lady's evening dress, and he in workman's clothes,
Dance across the shining water in wondrous, great repose.

They dance together as music plays and lilts across the lake
As they move across the water and leave a beautiful wake.

The music plays as moonlight streams across the painted night
Then strikes the hanging, vaunted stars to bring the sky alight.

They dance until the music fades, then sink beneath the waves
And all that's left is a mystery through all that wonder craves.

There is a peacefulness of evening time and stillness of the water.
Gone are the rustic workman and the socialite's pretty daughter.

While standing on McDonald's shore and looking at the lake,
Remember the flaming fireplace where embers fall and flake.

While you watch the lake at night, it's much more than it seems,
For it's made of haunting memories and vast, romantic dreams.

The End

Photo Credits

Glacier National Park Archives
Caption information for images requested by Gordon Butler
Note: All images should be credited as follows unless otherwise noted:
"Photos courtesy of Glacier National Park Archives."

HPF 2220: Lake McDonald Lodge Lobby, ca. 1920. Photograph by T. J. Hileman.
HPF 2222: Lake McDonald Lodge Dining Room, ca. 1920. Photograph by T. J. Hileman.
HPF 2223: Fireplace in lobby of Lake McDonald Lodge, ca. 1920. Photograph by T. J. Hileman.
HPF 2532: Lake McDonald Lodge, ca. 1920. Photograph by H.W. Hutchings.
HPF 2981: Lake McDonald Lodge, ca. 1915. Photograph by R. E. "Ted" Marble.

Made in the USA
Columbia, SC
19 June 2019